GOING TO THE PARISH
Mortlake and the Parish Church of
St Mary The Virgin

D1208214

MORTLAKE CHURCH, S.W.

1827

Ground Plan.

Scale of 10   50   100 feet

The Church and Church Path, 1827. (Lithographed by Charles Burton.)

GOING TO THE PARISH
Mortlake and the Parish Church of St Mary The Virgin

by
LESLIE FREEMAN

© Barnes & Mortlake History Society
1993

© Barnes and Mortlake History Society 1993
First published in 1993
by Barnes and Mortlake History Society
and
Picton Publishing (Chippenham) Limited
ISBN 0 948251 72 7

Set in Linotype Pilgrim by
Mike Kelly Phototypesetting,
Biddestone, Chippenham, Wiltshire SN14 7EA
Printed and Bound in the United Kingdom by
Picton Publishing (Chippenham) Limited
Queensbridge Cottages,
Patterdown,
Chippenham,
Wiltshire SN15 2NS
Telephone: (0249) 443430

All rights reserved
No part of this publication may be reproduced,
stored in a retrieval system or transmitted, in any form
or by any means, electronic, mechanical, photocopying,
recording or otherwise without the express written
permission of the copyright owners.

CONTENTS

LIST OF PLANS

LIST OF ILLUSTRATIONS

Front and Back Covers: The Parish Church as it is today

Unless otherwise acknowledged, the illustrations are from the Parish Church Print Collection (by kind permission of the Rector and Churchwardens) and from the author's collection.

FOREWORD

What is a church? Is it the building or a community of people? The more ancient and beautiful the building, the harder this dilemma becomes.

A church which has stood for centuries is a witness to the eternal nature of the Christian Gospel and can be a home for the faith, the memories, the joys and sorrows of a whole community. But it can become as cold and lifeless as stone. It needs the warmth and humanity of people to remind us that the Gospel is also about development, change and transformation.

Happily, we are not faced with this dilemma at Mortlake. The church building itself is almost a living thing. As Leslie Freeman vividly shows, ever since its foundation on its present site in 1543, the church has been in almost constant change, responding to the rising and falling fortunes of Mortlake, to passing architectural fashions and to changing theological convictions. It is impossible to tell the story of Mortlake Church without telling the story of its people. And that is just as it should be.

Leslie Freeman writes with the authority of someone who has known and loved Mortlake Church for many years. His very readable history is based on his own original research and builds on the work of other local historians. It is the first comprehensive modern history of the church and, knowing that it will be of immense value to future historians, visitors and worshippers, I am delighted to welcome its publication in this historic 450th anniversary year.

Bruce Saunders
Rector in the Mortlake with East Sheen Team Ministry

OUTLINE PLAN SHOWING THE DEVELOPMENT OF THE CHURCH

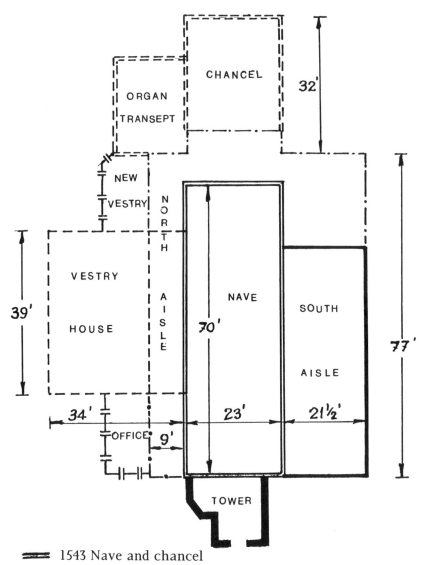

≡≡≡ 1543 Nave and chancel
--- c.1670 Vestry house incorporating north aisle
——— 1725 South aisle
—•— 1816 Extension to north aisle
—·— 1840 Nave, side aisles and chancel extended
≡≡≡ 1885 Chancel and organ transept
1906 Nave and side aisles rebuilt on foundations of 1840 church
⊣⊢ 1980 Additions

INTRODUCTION

This has not been an easy book to write. Perhaps no book is, but there are a number of factors which have made the task one of unexpected difficulty. I refer in the narrative to the exceptional nature of the Mortlake church records in both quality and quantity, but this only applies from the sixteenth century onwards. In contrast, our knowledge of earlier ages is meagre in the extreme and bedevilled by what I consider are dubious assumptions. I suggest in the opening chapter a rather different explanation of events, but a fuller discussion of the medieval period will only be possible when we have a better understanding of the documentary evidence and archaeological research to support it.

After the sixteenth century the problems are the sheer size of the archives available and the complexity caused by the frequent rebuilding of the church. Much has had to be omitted to avoid making the account overlong and rather tedious for the general reader. However, the Society has decided that the full text will be published in a limited edition and lodged in the parish records, the Surrey Record Office and the local libraries, so making my researches available to those who may wish to follow up some aspect of the parish or church history in greater detail.

The book is the culmination of many years of research, my interest and love of Mortlake and its church owing much to the influence of three notable past parishioners and members of the Society, Fred Mattingley, Henry Shearman and Charles Hailstone. More immediately, I am indebted to Mrs Maisie Brown (my successor as Chairman of the Society), Miss Mary Grimwade, and the Rev. Bruce Saunders for many helpful suggestions; to Mr David Catford for the excellent plan of the church, to Mrs Valerie Knight for preparing the index and Miss Judy Walker for not only proof-reading the text, but also for her many constructive criticisms. Two people deserve my special thanks. Firstly, Mr Raymond Gill. Any book on Mortlake would be the poorer without his profound knowledge of the parish and his unrivalled collection. Both have been placed unstintingly at my disposal and many were the hours spent in his study discussing my queries. Secondly, my wife Pamela for her forbearance over many months. Her patience must have been sorely tried by a husband who seemed to prefer the attractions of a word processor and who left tables groaning under the weight of documents and books.

Finally a word concerning the title. To past generations St Mary's was always the Parish Church and parishioners in general conversation always referred to it as such. Thus a typical greeting would be 'Going to the Parish Church?', or, quite simply, 'Going to the Parish?'

Leslie Freeman

A View of Mortlake up the Thames. Drawn and engraved by John Boydell, 1753. It is the earliest reliable view of Mortlake. The house on the right stands on the site of John Dee's house. Next to it are the Queen's Head and the former tapestry house, separated by an alley to the river which still exists. On the extreme left is The Limes, with its garden stretching along the riverbank.

1. THE EARLY CHURCH AND PARISH

There is a mention of Mortlake in the reign of Edward the Confessor (1042–66) in connection with a fishery which passed into the hands of the Archbishop of Canterbury, but, as with so many English villages, the first definite information comes in the Domesday survey of 1086. This states that Mortlake was held by the archbishop, and from its details we gather it was a relatively prosperous manor of about 8,000 acres, covering Mortlake, Barnes, Putney, Roehampton and Wimbledon. It would seem about half this area was arable land. No other part of the manor is mentioned except Barnes, which was granted to the Dean and Chapter of St Paul's by King Athelstan (924–39), and was for the most part independent of the rest of the manor, although paying taxes with Mortlake. There is no mention of a church at Barnes, but one is mentioned in the entry for Mortlake. Numbers of villagers, smallholders and slaves are listed, but these represent services due to the lord of the manor rather than the actual number of inhabitants. It probably indicates about 400–500 people

In the absence of any archaeological research, we cannot be certain but it seems logical to assume that the village grew up around the archbishop's manor house which is known to have stood east of Ship Lane on the site now covered by the old part of the brewery. Together with the church, this would have been the only building of any permanence for even the best medieval cottage would have been a mere hovel. It is reasonable to assume the church stood near the manor house, but historians have made much play that it was at Wimbledon because of a royal licence of Edward III in 1348. Edward made several visits to Mortlake while his friend John Stratford was archbishop, one such visit being in March 1348. Soon after that visit the King granted Stratford as lord of the manor a licence for the erection of a chapel on a piece of ground in Berecroft 'for the ease of the bodies and saving of the souls of the tenants of Estchene and Mortelak, who are far distant from their parish church'. This led Lysons[1] in the eighteenth century to assume the Domesday church was at Wimbledon, a supposition that later historians have followed without giving it the critical examination it deserves. Indeed some have waxed lyrical picturing the poor peasants of Mortlake walking the five miles to the church at Wimbledon.[2]

There are a number of serious objections to the supposition. It implies Mortlake was a place of little importance, whereas the evidence of the centuries following the Norman Conquest is quite to the contrary. Whilst the archbishops were not continuously in residence, there are numerous references to visits by them.

1   Daniel Lysons, *The Environs of London*, 1791–6.
2   Notably Horace Monroe, *Church Extension at Mortlake*, 1914, pp. 3–4. In fairness to Canon Monroe, he was not so much writing a history of the Parish Church as justifying the building of a new church.

Anselm was here at Whitsuntide in 1095, William de Corbeil was ill during a stay in 1136, John Peckham dated letters from here in 1281 and died here in 1292, as did Walter Reynolds in 1327, and Simon Meopham was in residence for some time in 1330. Not only that, in an age when the archbishop was as much a political as a religious figure, the monarch himself was also a visitor. King John came in March 1206, Edward II in 1316 and there are several references to visits by Edward III. This suggests that Mortlake was a place of some importance and it is difficult to conceive that successive archbishops left their own villagers without a church. Religion was too important a part of medieval village life for that to have happened, as is shown in Barnes where there was a church by 1100 even though Domesday suggests it was quite a small village.[3] Indeed, the existence of that church renders ridiculous the notion that the people of Mortlake walked five miles to Wimbledon for their church. The complete absence of evidence for a track between the two, not even the tradition of a greenway, is perhaps even stronger evidence against the theory. There is nothing at Wimbledon to corroborate the theory, and unfortunately neither there nor at Mortlake has any archaeological research been possible. Until there has been some such research, we can only surmise, but there must be the possibility that the licence referred to a settlement that was growing away from the main village. This settlement may well have disappeared in the Black Death, which first struck in 1349 and which it has been estimated may have halved the population by the end of the century. Lastly, there is the integrity of Domesday itself. It has been proved remarkably accurate and very strong evidence is needed to prove the church was anywhere but where it says it was, at Mortlake.

After the obscurities of 1348 it is a relief to get back to firmer ground, although between then and 1536 there is only one entry directly referring to the church. In 1383 Archbishop Courtney presented a piece of land for use as a burial ground, presumably enlarging an existing graveyard. Mortlake continued to see many notable occasions as archbishops and sovereigns came and went. For example, in 1406 Archbishop Thomas Arundel, assisted by the Bishops of Winchester and Worcester, consecrated Nicholas Bubwith Bishop of London. How much such events impinged on village life we cannot tell. Possibly very little, since a bishop's consecration would almost certainly have taken place in the archbishop's private chapel in the manor house. Nevertheless, prelates and monarchs travelled with a considerable retinue and the arrival of the King in particular must have affected the village. However, the accession of Henry VIII marked the end of Mortlake's long association with the archbishops, for in 1536 Thomas Cranmer was induced to give the manor to the King in exchange for other lands. Thus came to an end what was undoubtedly the most glamorous period in the history of Mortlake.

3   The fact that a church is not shown in a Domesday entry does not necessarily imply there was not one.

2. THE TUDOR CHURCH

Even before 1536 there had been great changes in the manor, brought about by the growing importance of Wimbledon. There is not much evidence for Wimbledon before the thirteenth century, but during that century its importance grew to the extent that it gave its name to the manor. Immediately after Henry VIII acquired the manor, he granted it to his Secretary of State, Thomas Cromwell, a native of Putney. Cromwell lost no time in making extensive alterations to the manor house, but he had little time to enjoy his new house for in 1540 he fell from grace and was beheaded. The manor reverted to the King, who in 1543 granted it to his sixth wife, Catherine Parr, but the grant did not include the manor house, which Henry reserved for his own use. The distance by river from Hampton Court to London was too great to be rowed in one day and Mortlake provided a convenient overnight stopping-place. We have no record of Henry himself using the house, but it was used by state visitors, for example the new French ambassador in 1546. The following year Henry died and the illustrious years of the house ended abruptly. There is no evidence that the later Tudor monarchs used it, and by then the close connection between church and house had been broken by the removal of the church to another site. The subsequent history of the manor and the old house is quickly summarized.

When Catherine Parr died in 1548 the manor reverted to the monarch and was in royal hands during most of Elizabeth's reign until in 1576 it was granted to Sir Thomas Cecil, son of the 1st Lord Burghley. He rebuilt the grange at Wimbledon, which became a mansion of great renown, completely overshadowing the old manor house by the river. From Sir Thomas the manor passed through several hands until in 1717 it was purchased by Sir Theodore Janssen, a director of the South Sea Company, who, faced with financial problems after the 'South Sea Bubble' burst in 1720, sold it to Sarah, Duchess of Marlborough. She bequeathed it to her favourite grandson, the Hon. John Spencer, and it has remained in the Spencer family to the present day. The old manor house is last recorded as being occupied in the late seventeenth century, and it was demolished some time during the eighteenth.

Why Henry VIII ordered the removal of the church to its present site in 1543 is not recorded; possibly it impeded alterations being made to the old house. The new site was only about a quarter of a mile to the east, but it brought the church quite close to the boundary with Barnes. The subsequent expansion of the village away from the river has thus left it on the periphery of the parish. The reason for it being placed where it is may puzzle us, but it was close to the centre of the village and the field path we know as Church Path gave an excellent route to East Sheen. It is impossible to know how the village grew in the centuries after Domesday, but a survey dating from the mid-sixteenth century suggests that the village was still largely centred in the area of Thames Bank, Ship Lane, the Green and the western part of the High Street, with settlements southwards in East Sheen and a large house at West Hall. A clearer picture emerges from a survey some fifty years later, in 1618,[1] which confirms that the main village lay along the riverside, but also shows dwellings around Milestone Green[2] and along Sheen Lane and Christ Church Road. Of the seventy-six dwellings it listed, a third were in East Sheen, and of the total acreage over half was owned by five people, four of whom lived in East Sheen.[3] Clearly, East Sheen was increasingly where the wealthier residents lived. Church Path gave them a direct route to the church; 450 years later it remains a well-used route, and for half the distance it is still a footpath. The railway upset its course, but had first to provide a crossing and then a bridge. Later, when Church Avenue was laid out, the path on the east side was laid exactly on the course of the old footpath. The site may have seemed an admirable one in 1543, for the existing complex of footpaths probably made it difficult to find a site nearer Sheen Lane and the Green, whereas the area to the east and south of the church remained fields until the early years of this century.

The notable feature of the rebuilding of the church is that it appears to have been by direct order of the King. The royal accounts for 1543 and 1544 show payments to the Paymaster of the King's Works for work carried out at Hampton Court, Nonsuch, Oatlands and Mortlake, to be 'employed upon the payment of wages of masons, carpenters, sawers, bricklayers, and all other manner artificers'.[4] Unfortunately, detailed accounts for these works have not been found, but in the seventeenth century Richard Symmes, the town clerk of Guildford, wrote a history of Surrey. He obtained much of his information by going from parish to parish, questioning the local people. Of Mortlake he wrote:

> Mortlake is a parish upon the River Thames between
> Barn-elmes and Shene or Richmond. The kings of England
> have formerly had a standing house here, near unto which
> stood the Church which was afterwards removed to the
> place where it now standeth by King Henry VIII, Anno
> domini 1543.

Richard Jeffree[5] also alluded to the evidence of eighteenth-century visitors to Mortlake, whose interest lay in the tapestry works but who found the locals obsessed by the fact that Henry VIII had built their church.

Unfortunately, nothing remains of the 1543 church except the tower, but a number of points tend to confirm the story. Firstly, the tower is not immediately

1   The survey was carried out for Thomas Cecil, Earl of Exeter, then lord of the manor.
2   Milestone Green, the crossroads in Sheen Lane. In general, modern road names are used.
3   The origin of East Sheen is obscure. The name derives from Shene, the old name of Richmond which was changed by decree of Henry VII in 1498. In the earliest records it is referred to as a hamlet of Mortlake and its boundaries have never been defined. It is generally agreed to cover the area south of the Upper Richmond Road, but there is a 'grey' area between that road and the railway.
4   Unpublished research notes by Caroline Crimp, in the records of the Barnes & Mortlake History Society.
5   Richard Jeffree, *The Story of Mortlake Churchyard*, Barnes & Mortlake History Society, 1983.

recognizable as a Tudor structure; the lower three storeys are more typical of the fifteenth century and a careful examination of the stone shows it to be re-used material, an opinion confirmed by a member of the Surrey Archaeological Society some years ago. Secondly, there is the construction of the tower, with foundations so deep that they provided the Victorians with a ready-made boiler-house. This is in contrast to St Mary's, Barnes, for example, where the tower built some sixty years earlier has very slight foundations. It suggests the tower was built by masons who were more able and experienced than one would expect to find in a village such as Mortlake. Thirdly, a commemorative stone in the west front of the tower is inscribed:

VIVAT

RH8

1543

(Long Live Henry VIII)

One can imagine the local parishioners inserting the stone to flatter the King, but if they had been coerced into moving the church it is unlikely it would have survived long after his death. Not only did it survive, when it became worn a new stone was inserted and the remains of the old one were inserted into the west wall of the south aisle. While none of this evidence is conclusive, it does tend to point to a royal involvement. The little church has another claim to fame. The Act of Supremacy marking the final break with Rome was passed in 1534, so the rebuilding of Mortlake church only nine years later makes it one of the earliest churches built for the newly independent Church of England

Because so little of the Tudor church survives, our knowledge of it is very limited. John Aubrey[6] mentions a stone above the east window inscribed:

AR

HS

1543

All our other knowledge has to be deduced from plans which, although of later date, show the ground-plan of the church, together with a few engravings and drawings made before the last remnants of the old nave and church were demolished. They enable us with reasonable certainty to conclude the church had an undivided nave and chancel, 70 feet long and 23 feet wide, aisle-less, and stone-built in the distinctive ashlar and flint still visible in the lower storeys of the tower. Substantial buttresses at the east end matched those on the tower at the west end; these were almost certainly purely decorative if the nave had similar foundations to those of the tower.

Since the new church was a reconstruction, it is not unreasonable to surmise it was of similar form to the old one, although cut stone strongly suggests the latter

---

6 John Aubrey, *A Perambulation of the County of Surrey; Begun 1673, Ended 1692,* 1718.

was rebuilt in the fifteenth century. Until transport improved towards the end of the fourteenth century, the use of stone was largely confined to districts where workable stone was easily available. It was not until the fifteenth century that it began to be used more generally, often in association with additions by wealthy benefactors. The engravings and drawings show that the chancel was ashlar-faced, together with a surviving portion of the north wall. If this is indicative of the whole original building, then Mortlake had a more handsome church than we have imagined for it was rare for a church to be completely ashlar-faced. Inserted in the Tudor brickwork of the turret on the north side of the tower is a stone inscribed '1407', which must have been of some significance for it to be kept by the builders of 1543. Possibly it refers to such a rebuilding but, like so much else associated with the church, this must remain only a conjecture.

MORTLAKE, SURREY.

Pub. March 28.1807. by S.Woodburn 112.St Martins Lane London

Mortlake Church c. 1795. Engraved from a wash drawing by S. Woodburn. Of great interest as it shows the church in its surroundings and the tower in its original state. Note the small chuchyard (it was enlarged in 1799) with its low wall and stile across Church Path.

3. THE SEVENTEENTH CENTURY

The Dedication

The dedication to St Mary the Virgin no doubt dates back to the Domesday church, but it seems to be one that was rarely used before the introduction of the team ministry in 1976. Until then it was invariably referred to as the Parish Church. Not only is this a strong vernacular tradition, there is little in the vestry records to indicate a use of the dedication before about 1850. Even a faculty in 1724 from the Archbishop of Canterbury for the enlargement of the church is addressed to 'the Minister, Churchwardens and People of the Parish of Mortlake' and the 'Parish Church of Mortlake', with no reference to a dedication. Because of its long use, the historic style of the Parish Church will be followed in this history.

The First Enlargement

It seems a gallery was added late in the sixteenth century, presumably at the west end of the nave, but the first major alteration to the Tudor church was in 1637 when there was an expenditure of no less that £176.6s.1d. on 'reparatione and beautifyinge of the Church'. Exactly what this entailed is not known, except that 'Mr William Leachland seated the Chancell and Church at a cost to himself personally of £45.10s.0d.' and a rate of £151.16s.6d. was laid on the parish. This latter figure included the gift of William Leachland, so the cost of the work exceeded the rate by a considerable margin; since William Leachland paid for the new pews, we are left wondering what the balance of over £130 was spent on. Possibly it was in connection with the addition of the north aisle and vestry house.

The building of the vestry house is generally linked with a vestry minute dated 7 April 1534 which states that, in consideration of the parish allowing him to enclose all the land within Clay Ends, John Blackwell[1] would pay 20 marks (£13.33s.) with a promise to pay a further 20 nobles (£6.16s.) when a schoolhouse was built. Nothing more is recorded until 25 September 1670, when the Vestry resolved that the new building on the north side of the church be converted into a dwelling house for the minister 'for ever'. A month later, on 31 October, the resolution was rescinded, the entry struck out in the minute book, and a further resolution passed to the effect that the building should be a schoolhouse.

That is the limit of information in the vestry minutes, but in the records of the Dean and Chapter of Worcester there is a grant made in November 1670 to the

1 John Blackwell was a grocer who lived at old Cromwell House and is first recorded in the rate book for 1626. Elected to the Vestry in 1628, he was active in parish affairs for the following twenty years at least. The minutes record him at various times to have been an overseer of the poor, surveyor of highways and auditor. He was a man of some substance, gave several gifts to the church and in 1656 was High Sheriff of Surrey. A royalist, he changed sides early in the Civil War and in 1645 was made a captain in the parliamentary army. He died in 1658. (His son John also lived at Cromwell House and had a similar career in the parliamentary army.)

parish of Mortlake concerning a building adjacent to the church which was intended to be a schoolhouse but which had not been completed and had fallen into decay. The grant allowed the parish to complete the building as a house for the minister. This seems to confirm the date of completion of the vestry house as 1670, but leaves unclear the date that construction began and its relationship with the north aisle. That the latter was built before 1670 is certain, for in that year the vestry minutes refer to a new gallery being built in it. Plans from the early part of the nineteenth century show the aisle within the house, but a separate entity with a wall between them. It must have been built at the same time as the house and this seems to be the most likely explanation of the large expenditure in 1637. Unfortunately, the churchwardens' account detailed in the minutes provides no insight into the work carried out; the principal item of £60 reads 'pd the Joyner for his worcke as appeerth by his bill in full'. Presumably the start of the Civil War prevented completion of the house.

Why the Vestry decided in 1670 to complete the house as a residence for the minister and so quickly changed its mind is a mystery. It was almost certainly never used as a clergy house, although we know nothing about its use as a school. Presumably it was the charity school which in 1721 received bequests from Edward Colston and Lady Dorothy Capel of Kew. The long history of that school is outside the scope of this account, except in so far as it was carried on in the upper room of the house until about 1815. The first recorded meeting of the Vestry in the lower room of the house is in June 1676, which in due time led to the house being called the vestry room or house.

The church, c. 1814. The top stage of the tower was reconstructed in 1796, but the north aisle has not been extended westwards and a portion of the original Tudor north wall is shown, together with the vestry house completed in 1670.

8

4. THE CHURCH AND PARISH, 1700–1840

It is with some relief that we reach the eighteenth century, for not only are the vestry records at their most informative but we have the first engravings and drawings. Some of them are of doubtful accuracy and they do not show many of the features we would like to see, but the work of John Boydell, J. L. Chatelain, W. Foster and S. H. Grimm from the 1750s onwards gives us a good picture of the church, at least on the outside, and of Mortlake itself.

The Parish

The old village was still predominantly clustered around the alleyways radiating off the High Street, the Green, Ship Lane and Thames Bank. East of the church were open fields, although some large houses were built on the river side of the High Street. (A few still survive, for example The Limes.) Opposite the church the tapestry works, whose high-quality tapestries made the name of Mortlake known throughout Europe, had opened in 1619. It was never a successful venture financially and it closed in 1703, parts of the site being sold and built over during the following years. The tapestry works had an important religious effect on Mortlake. Flemish weavers were brought over when the works opened, and inter-marriage with local families was the most likely reason why Mortlake had a large and notable dissenting congregation as early as the seventeenth century. After the closure of the tapestry works, the main industries in the village were probably brewing and pottery. Brewing had no doubt gone on for centuries in small breweries along the river bank, but in the nineteenth century these small breweries merged into one large brewery. The first pottery works opened in the middle of the eighteenth century and the industry was to last about a hundred years. There were two pottery works at different periods, both producing salt-glaze stoneware. The products were strictly utilitarian, but are now collectors' items. Members of both the families who owned the pottery works, Sanders and Kishere, are buried in the churchyard and in the church itself is a display of items from the later Kishere factory.

Moving away from the old village southwards along Sheen Lane were some large houses and a few clusters of cottages. East Sheen between Upper Richmond Road and the Park was characterized by large mansions and estates, for it was a country retreat for City magnates. (Alderman John Barber and Sir Philip Francis are examples.) Temple Grove and East Sheen Lodge on the west side of Sheen Lane and Sheen House and Palewell Lodge on the east side were among the largest and most important. However, perhaps the most notable feature of the parish were the market gardens. These came into being during the seventeenth century and were at their zenith during the nineteenth, supplying fresh fruit and vegetables to London. They covered a great part of the parish, particularly west of

9

Sheen Lane on both sides of the Upper Richmond Road. They also had a religious effect on Mortlake as they employed much casual labour, especially Irish Roman Catholics in the early nineteenth century. It was probably they who formed part of a growing congregation which led to the building of St Mary Magdalene Roman Catholic church on a site immediately south of the Parish Church in 1852.

The Church – the Age of the Pew

After an enlargement early in the century, the church stood with few changes for nearly a hundred years, by which time overcrowding was a serious problem. The population of the parish had been fairly stable at about 1,800 for much of the eighteenth century, but began to rise early in the nineteenth. In addition, a prime reason for the problem was the Georgian box pew. Before the seventeenth century the nave probably had little more than a few benches but, after the changes under the Tudors and the Commonwealth, preaching was the dominant feature of the service. Sermons were long, at least an hour, and this had a dramatic effect on church furnishings. The pulpit with its sounding board was placed high so that all could hear and the nave was crammed with galleries and high-sided box pews, the latter to give a little comfort from the cold in the draughty and unheated church. It was still usual for everyone to attend the Sunday services and the problem of space arose through pews being allotted and paid for by individual parishioners.

Each local family had its own pew which, once allotted, no one else could use, even when the owners were away, thus severely limiting the number of free seats. It also caused disputes. After the restoration of the church in 1725, the subscribers were allotted pews in consideration of their gifts. In 1741 the Vestry ordered that allotted pews did not belong to the houses where the subscribers lived, and in 1743 it ordered that no family should have two pews and that partitions must not be removed. Nevertheless, as late as 1805 an advertisement in *The Times* concerning the sale of a house in East Sheen referred to 'a handsome pew in Mortlake Church' as one of its perquisites. Finally in 1833 the Vestry resolved to take counsel's opinion as to whether pew-holders had the right to lock their pews to the exclusion of the churchwardens! (No record survives whether they received such an opinion.) The pews were a considerable source of income and for some years they were put up for auction. In June 1757 a Mr Seward offered two guineas for a pew, an offer the Vestry accepted, and in May 1746 Theodore Eccleston paid twenty guineas for the pew of the late Alderman John Barber.

1700–1840

In September 1721, the Vestry resolved to enlarge the church and a subscribers' list was taken round, it seems without much support initially for it was not until July 1724 that the Vestry gave its consent and a faculty was obtained. A minute dated 27 June 1725 states:

S. MARY'S, MONKLAKE.

Shewing Pews & Names of Occupiers in 1836.

The Galleries in 1836 & Names of Occupiers.

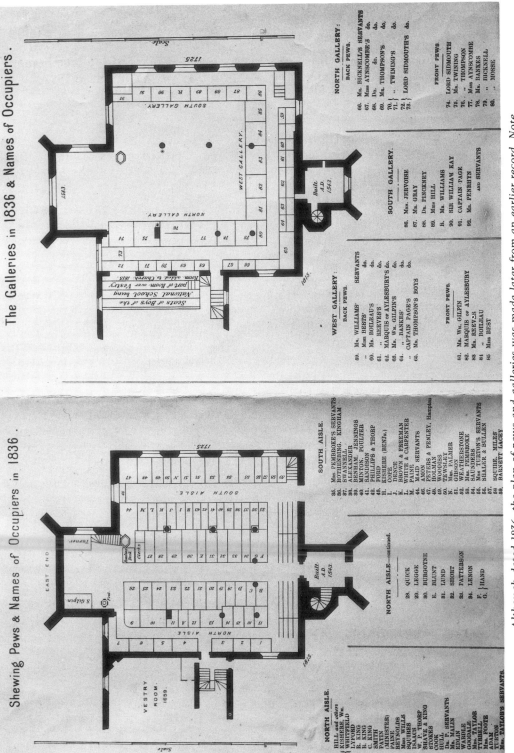

NORTH AISLE.
1. HILL and others
2. KUSHER, Wm.
3. WHITFIELD
4. LYFORD
5. R. KING
6. R. KING
7. C. KING
8. SMITH
9. PATIN
10. (MINISTER)
11. PAINE
A. REYNOLDS
12. Mrs. WILLS
13. SQUIRES
14. ISAACS
15. W. THORP
16. SLEVE & KING
17. STOKES
R. COOK
C. HULL
D. HULL'S SERVANTS
18. Mr. MALIN
19. EDLIN
20. WARDLE
21. GOODALE
22. Mr. TAYLOR
23. TYRRELL
24. Mrs. FOOTE
25. ADAM
26. BURTON
27. Mrs. TAYLOR'S SERVANTS.

NORTH AISLE—continued.
28. QUICK
29. LEGGE
30. BURGOYNE
E. BLUNT
31. LUND
32. SHORT
33. PATTERSON
34. LENON
F. } HAND
G. }

SOUTH AISLE.
35. Mrs. PEMBROKE'S SERVANTS
36. ROTHENBURG. KINGHAM
87. SWANNELL
88. ALEXANDER
89. BENHAM. JENNINGS
40. MINTON. FOULGER
41. SANDISON
42. PHILLIPS & THORP
43. FORD
H. KISSERE (BENJ.)
I. COPE
J. DENCE
K. BROWN & FREEMAN
L. WHITE & CARPENTER
M. PAINE
44. MAID SERVANTS
45. AMON
46. PETERS & PENLEY, Hampton
47. HOLMAN
48. WOODISS
49. TEWSLEY
N. Mrs. PALMER
50. GIBSON
61. WEATHERSTONE
62. Mrs. PEMBROKE
64. SAUNDERS
65. Mrs. TURTON'S SERVANTS
67. SHALER & BULLEN
68. SQUIRE. MILES
69. BARNETT LACEY

WEST GALLERY:
BACK PEWS.
60. Mr. WILLIAMS' SERVANTS
" Mrs. BEST'S do.
60. Mr. BOILEAU'S do.
61. " REEVES'S do.
62. MARQUIS or AYLESBURY'S do.
63. Mr. Wm. GILPIN'S do.
64. " BANKES' do.
" CAPTAIN PAGE'S do.
65. Mr. THOMPSON'S BOYS do.

FRONT PEWS.
81. Mr. Wm. GILPIN
82. MARQUIS or AYLESBURY
83. Mr. REEVES
84. " BOILEAU
85 Miss BEST

SOUTH GALLERY.
86. Mrs. JERVOISE
87. Mr. GRAY
88. Dr. PINCKNEY
89. Miss HILL
R. Mr. WILLIAMS
90. SIR WILLIAM KAY
91. CAPTAIN PAGE
92. Mr. PENRHYN
and SERVANTS

NORTH GALLERY:
BACK PEWS.
66. Mr. BICKNELL'S SERVANTS
67. Miss AYNSCOMBE'S do.
68. Do. do.
69. Mr. THOMPSON'S do.
71. } .. TWINING'S
72. } LORD SIDMOUTH'S do.

FRONT PEWS.
74. LORD SIDMOUTH
75. Mr. TWINING
76. " THOMPSON
77. Miss AYNSCOMBE
78. Mr. BANKES
79. " BICKNELL
80. " MOSSE

Although dated 1836, the plan of pews and galleries was made later from an earlier record. Note the pew in each corner of the chancel.

> Waterman's Gallery to be taken down and rebuilt, and pews north side of middle ile to be new built and ile and cross ile repaired with stone, and door to be made at north side and old font to be removed and new one placed in ile.

Fortunately this last decision was later rescinded. The Waterman's gallery was at the west end of the nave but the principal work, the building of the south aisle, is not mentioned in the minute. However, it is detailed in the faculty. As built, the aisle was 53 feet by 21½ feet (internal dimensions), with the roof and gallery supported on three columns and access to the latter from a staircase in the south-west corner. There were four windows on the south side, another in the east wall and a door and porch in the west wall with a round light above. Later drawings show that it was built in red brick, with a steeply pitched roof like the nave, and that there was a sundial midway along the south wall.

Subscribers to the work included the 1st Lord Palmerston who lived at Temple Grove, Sir Gerard Conyers who was Lord Mayor of London in 1723, and Alderman John Barber who was to be Lord Mayor in 1733 and who had recently bought East Sheen Lodge as his summer residence. The most notable subscriber, however, was the King. Representations were made to him since part of the parish was in New Park (now Richmond Park), which was a royal park. George I:

> . . . out of his great bounty, was graciously pleased to give One Hundred Pounds towards beautifying the said church, to bee paid to, and disposed of by, the Right Honble Henry Lord Viscount Palmerston.

In 1816–17 a further, small enlargement was made involving the extension of the north aisle the full length of the nave at the west end, new galleries and enlarging the existing north gallery by taking in part of the upper floor of the vestry house. The architect was Charles King, who lived at Suthrey House in the High Street and was later to be Vestry Clerk. The cost was £1,200. The former Prime Minister, Henry Addington, 1st Lord Sidmouth, who lived at White Lodge, gave £100 and a church rate raised £785.10s., but a large part of the expense was met by the churchwarden Francis (later Sir Francis) Ommanney. Drawings made a few years later in the 1820s show a slender, rather spindly chimney sprouting from the west end of the south aisle, the first evidence of heating in the church. The drawings also show that the sundial had been removed.

These alterations destroyed a large part of the Tudor church, leaving only the chancel walls and the nave roof, but for all that the church assumed perhaps its most attractive aspect. The steeply pitched roofs and battlemented tower give it the aspect of a very pleasant country church, especially when viewed from the south-west over the low churchyard wall. Unfortunately, these changes failed to provide the additional seating necessary for the increasing congregation and in 1840 another, more ambitious rebuilding of the church was put in hand.

A Picture of the Church Around 1800

Drawings and paintings of the eighteenth-century church show what seems a very pleasant country church, but it is not until the 1790s that we have the first description of the interior and it is not very inspiring. It is taken from notes which appeared in 1807 when a print from a drawing by S. Woodburn was published. The drawing was actually made about 1795 and the notes presumably date from the same time:

> The present structure consists of a chancel, nave and two ailes, the roof of the nave being supported on wooden pillars, and cieled with plaster. The whole internal appearance having been compleatly modernized.

Anderson[1] quotes a description of 1830 when:

> . . . there were a few windows with flat arches, such as were in use in Henry VIIIs reign. The body of the church is brick and is exceedingly plain, the ceiling is flat, divided into panels and supported by Tuscan columns.

In fact, at that time the only Tudor windows which could have survived were in the walls of the chancel. In his other writings Anderson makes several references to the high pews, which included some large, square ones for notable parishioners such as the Duchess of Gloucester and Lord William Fitzroy. It is true he was writing after the rebuilding of 1840, but the pews pre-dated that enlargement. It is also recorded that in the chancel green curtains were draped around the east window, on the walls were boards with the Commandments, the Lord's Prayer and the Creed, the Royal Arms hung from the west gallery and the pews were kept locked. The comments, meagre though they are, give the impression that the church was not considered particularly attractive. A judgement is not possible, but the 'exceeding plain' of one age can be the 'simple and lovely' of a later.

To supplement the written word, there are several plans and a lithograph dating from the early nineteenth century. These show the church packed with pews right up to the small chancel; indeed there are pews on either side in the chancel itself. In the little space left, the font stands on the north side by the chancel with the high pulpit and clerk's desk opposite. The galleries were continuous round three sides of the nave, and were likewise crammed with pews, with the north gallery taking in part of the upper room of the vestry house. Access to the galleries was by stairs in the vestry house, in the north-west wall of the church and the south-west corner of the south aisle. The only free seats seem to have been under the west gallery. The lithograph is dated before the 1840 rebuilding and confirms

---

1 John Eustace Anderson, *A History of the Parish of Mortlake*, published privately 1883, facsimile edition Vade-Mecum Press 1983, pp. 16–17. (Anderson was the first historian of Mortlake and frequent reference will be made to his published and unpublished work in the following pages. A full list of his works will be found in the bibliography.)

the impression of the plans, with pews crowding up to the chancel and the pulpit towering above them. Prominent under the east window is the altar-piece 'The Entombment of Christ', but there is no sign of the two pews shown in the earlier plans nor of the declamatory boards; presumably they had already been removed. The curtains mentioned as being draped round the east window are shown, as are some of the memorials in their original positions. In particular, on the north wall the Godschall memorial is prominent, together with the one to Ursula, Lady Sidmouth, while just visible on the south wall is the Coventry memorial. The artist of this valuable drawing was Elizabeth Acworth Prinsep (1804–85), daughter of Sir Francis Ommanney, who was shortly to marry as her second husband the architect Samuel Beachcroft.

The chancel prior to the rebuilding of 1840. The earliest interior view of the church, it shows the alter-piece and various monuments in their original positions. (Engraved by J. M. Bayne from a drawing by Elizabeth Acworth Prinsep, daughter of Sir Francis Ommanney.)

Mortlake High Street from the east. Unfinished wash drawing dated October 1820 in the Paton Collection.

Mortlake, c. 1830. From a Lithograph by Charles King, drawing master at Miss Crabtree's school in East Sheen and Vestry Clerk 1828–1855. The bend of the river is exaggerated but it gives a lively impression of Mortlake at that time. The mansion on the left is Castlenau House which stood by the river opposite Ashleigh Road. The tapestry house and the Queen's Head are to the right of the mast of the sailing barge.

5. THE BEACHCROFT CHURCH, 1840-1885

The total seating in the church after the alterations of 1816 was 880, of which only ninety-eight were free. The rising population made an increase in free seating essential and in April 1838 the Vestry agreed to an enlargement, which went ahead in June 1840 to the designs of Samuel Beachcroft (c.1801–61). The builder was Thomas Long of Richmond. It was a considerable work, for the nave and south aisles were extended eastwards to their present extent of 77 feet, with a new but very shallow chancel only 5 feet deep. Thus the last vestiges of the Tudor church were destroyed. The south gallery was rebuilt, indeed the whole south aisle was probably rebuilt since it was extended at the east end, had six windows instead of four in the south wall and the porch at the west end was altered. Both nave and aisle were given flat roofs and the vestry house was also re-roofed. The old pews and fittings were retained, but rearranged. Plans show that most of nearly 400 new free seats were crammed under the south gallery, with some at the west end, and there were children's seats in both side aisles by the shallow chancel. The alterations increased the total seating to almost 1,300. The font was moved to the west end of the church. No picture of the rebuilt church survives, so we do not know what the chancel looked like, but we do know that the altar-piece was still in place and that there was a stucco dado (a rendering over the lower part of the walls). The new chancel was, however, so small that the monuments in the old chancel must have been moved to their present positions at this time. The cost of the work was nearly £2,700 and subscribers included the Archbishop of Canterbury, the Dean and Chapter of Worcester, Earl Spencer and Lord Sidmouth.

The rebuilding was successful in providing the extra seating required but in other respects it was an unmitigated disaster. Only ten years later nearly £600 had to be spent on more alterations and repairs. The stucco dado was swept away by the incumbent Swinny, who also banished the altar-piece to the vestry room. Instead he had oak panelling put round the sanctuary and installed a new altar and pulpit and stained glass in the east window (the first reference to stained glass at Mortlake). However, it was not only the taste and style of Beachcroft's work that caused concern. A letter dated October 1850 to Beachcroft from the churchwardens Francis Ommanney (son of Sir Francis) and Henry Bullen reads, 'all the pillars then put up by you are already so much decayed as to be pronounced unsafe'. Beachcroft defended himself by stating the difficulties he had had in obtaining large enough timbers to match the existing columns and of the problems judging whether such timbers were good. He also referred to the great speed in which he had been expected to complete the works to avoid closing the church longer than necessary. His opinion was that the problem had been caused by a leak from the gutters. It must have been rather embarrassing, for Francis Ommanney and Samuel Beachcroft were brothers-in-law!

Charles Lee of Golden Square, W1, was the architect who oversaw the repairs to make good Beachcroft's deficiencies, as well as installing heating and lighting for the first time. Gas lighting had been brought to Mortlake the previous year by the Brentford Gas Company, which laid pipes along the High Street and Sheen Lane. Leading the subscribers to this work was the Duchess of Gloucester, then residing at White Lodge, who gave 60 guineas. The new pulpit was presented by the Rev. Dr G. C. Rowden, headmaster of Temple Grove.

In the following years attempts were made to improve the church. The old box pews were replaced in 1866; the new pews were lower and in the neat rows beloved of Victorians, although they still had doors. In 1865–7 the gas lighting was improved, new altar rails were installed in 1873 and in 1880 the chancel was redecorated at the expense of James Wigan. Dissatisfaction with the church still festered, however, and in 1885 the present chancel was erected, the first stage in the building of the present church. The last words on Beachcroft's church come from 1905 when the nave was about to be rebuilt. The vicar, Walter Furneaux, described it as 'inconvenient, unsightly, dark and ill-ventilated', while the faculty for the rebuilding stated it was:

> . . . a comparatively modern structure belonging to the Georgian period and the structure is of a Debased design, absolutely devoid of a redeeming feature from an Antiquarian or Architectural point of view.
> . . . the galleries rendered the church exceedingly gloomy.

Any further comment is superfluous!

The church as rebuilt by Samuel Beachcroft in 1840. The lithograph is dated 1851.

The occasion is a match between Eton and Winchester rowed in August 1843, but it also depicts an unusually accurate view of the Mortlake riverfront. The three houses directly in front of the church are nos. 101, 103 and 105 Mortlake High Street. To the right stands the tapestry house and the Queen's Head. (From a lithograph by R. K. Thomas.)

6. THE BLOMFIELD CHURCH, 1885–1906

When the decision was made that a further rebuilding was necessary, it was natural that the architect the parish should turn to was Arthur William Blomfield (1829–99). He had built Christ Church, had lived in East Sheen and numbered many prominent local families among his friends. His father had been Bishop of London and, after studying architecture under Hardwick, he had acquired a wide ecclesiastical connection, although never achieving the status of one of the leading Victorian architects. Christ Church, one of his first church commissions, was built in a French Gothic style, but in later years a surfeit of 'Gothic' restorations stilted his style and he could seldom be persuaded to let his talents have free rein. Apart from Christ Church, the later Holy Innocents at High Beech in Epping Forest is an example of what he could achieve. His work was of a very high standard, as is exemplified by his nave of Southwark Cathedral. Besides Christ Church, completed in 1863, he also built The Cottage in Christ Church Road, where he lived from 1863 to 1869. (It still stands at the junction with Fife Road.) He was churchwarden at Christ Church, 1866–7, became an ARA in 1888 and was knighted in 1889.

In the light of his career, it is not surprising that Blomfield proposed rebuilding the church in the Early English style. It is clear from the later 1906 rebuilding appeal that he envisaged a grander church than in fact was built. Only the vestry house and tower were to be retained, and the latter was to have a new top stage with tall pinnacles at each corner. No doubt financial constraints restricted the initial rebuilding to the chancel. This was carried out in 1885. The foundation stone was laid on Whit Monday (25 May) by the Dean of Worcester and the completed work dedicated by the Bishop of Rochester on 25 November. The new chancel was the same width as the old, but extended to the eastern boundary of the churchyard; in fact, it forms part of the churchyard wall. It is a lofty conception, its height of 32 feet equalling its length, but the large chancel arch was partly obscured by the low roof of Beachcroft's nave. On the north side two arches give access to an organ transept, 22 feet long and 18 feet wide, and on the south side are two corresponding blind arches, which still await the side chapel of the original design. For this reason part of the outside wall was left in unrendered brick. The cost was about £2,500.

The church was to remain in this odd condition for twenty years with Blomfield's chancel in uneasy union with Beachcroft's nave. Fortunately there are several illustrations of the church in this condition and the Beachcroft nave does not look as bad as Furneaux and the faculty described it, although no contemporary writer had a good word for it. Soon after the turn of the century the condition of the nave roof began to cause increasing concern and it was this that brought about the next phase of Blomfield's church. A public meeting to consider a restoration or rebuilding of the nave was held in February 1903, and later a General Meeting of Parishioners resolved that a new nave be built and the south aisle rebuilt on the existing foundations, using as far as possible the old materials. An appeal was launched which made clear that the north aisle, side chapel, south porch and tower were excluded from the scheme. The estimated cost of the nave and south aisle was £6,198 and the wording of the appeal, 'that (if possible) a new Nave . . . be built', seems to strike a negative note, as if there were doubts about being able to raise the funds. As we shall see, there were to be difficulties. Since the architect had died in 1899, the rebuilding was entrusted to his firm, Sir Arthur Blomfield & Sons, but there seems no reason to doubt that they followed in broad outline the design Sir Arthur had prepared in 1885.

By 1904 sufficient funds had been raised to place a contract for the nave, and before work commenced other contracts were placed for the south aisle and porch, both to a simplified design. The church closed after services on Sunday, 30 April 1905 and the rebuilt church was dedicated by the Bishop of Southwark a year later on Saturday, 28 April 1906. The 1885 chancel was now joined to a nave of five bays, with a sixth half-sized bay at the west end, lighted by a lofty clerestory and with the arches springing from octagonal pillars without capitals at 14-feet centres. In its austere simplicity it is a noble creation, best viewed perhaps from the chancel. The opening of Christ Church and a changing pattern of church-going made it possible to dispense with galleries; the seating capacity of the new church, about 550, was less than half that of the old. The north aisle was left unchanged except that, with the removal of the gallery, the wall between the church and vestry house was restored. (It had been removed when the gallery was extended into the upper room of the vestry house in 1816.) The south aisle was given a lead-covered lean-to roof, with a porch facing the churchyard replacing the one at the west end. As it was anticipated that the side chapel would be the next stage of the rebuilding, the east wall of the 1840 aisle was retained, with the window blocked on the inside. The fittings of the earlier church, notably the pews of 1866, were retained but an improvement which was probably much appreciated was the replacement of gas lighting by electricity.

The builders were Joseph Dorey & Co. Ltd. of Brentford and their invoice was £4,452.13s.6d. out of a total cost of £5,098.1s.4d.[1] The financial position, however, was not satisfactory. When work commenced the appeal stood at £3,400, a year later with the church completed it stood at only £4,000, and it was 1908 before the deficit was cleared. This was only part of the problem. During the year that the church was closed, baptisms and services of Holy Communion were held in the upper room of the vestry house and Sunday morning and evening services in the large hall at the Wigan Institute. The arrangements should have worked well enough in the circumstances, but the parish reports show that financially they were disastrous. Offertories barely covered the churchwardens' expenses and the situation was made worse by a drop of 25 per cent in the collections at Christ Church between 1904 and 1906. Since these had for many years considerably

1 The actual amount varies according to source. This figure comes from the final account in the parish report, 1908.

exceeded those of the Parish Church, the effect on the parish finances must have been severe. This may explain the caution of the appeal committee and also the decision of the vicar, Walter Furneaux, to resign in 1909 in favour of a younger man when the rebuilding debt had been cleared.

The parish reports published each year until the 1920s detailed the contributors to the myriad of funds which supported the church and some of the less fortunate in the parish. The list of contributions to the restoration appeal shows there were over 200 and that the majority were quite modest. The principal gift was 1,000 guineas from Mrs James Wigan and family, with smaller amounts from other members of the Wigan family. These and a number of other gifts were given specifically in memory of James Wigan and the nave was therefore rebuilt in his memory. Among the smaller contributors, the Cromwell House servants (James Wigan's residence) gave £2.3s.10d. and 'The Vicar's Old Nurse' 3 guineas. The brewers, Watney, Combe, Reid & Co., gave £50, Viscount Sidmouth £10 and the Mayor of Richmond 2 guineas. A considerable contribution was made by events such as £225 from a 'Prize Contest and Competition Sale', £390 from a bazaar, £68 from social evenings, and £50 apiece from a garden fête and 'White Tableaux and Japanese Operetta'. Last, but not least, was 'Parish Marmalade £95.11s.6d.' In the years before the 1914 war ladies in the parish made marmalade which was sold for various worthy causes, but to raise nearly £100 in 1905 suggests some very industrious ladies, besides being a commentary on the amount of marmalade consumed in Mortlake at the time!

Interior of the church c. 1899 showing the Beachcroft nave of 1840 and the Blomfield chancel of 1885. The figure is reputed to be that of George Falla, who was parish clerk for over thirty years from 1890.

7. THE CHURCH SINCE 1906

The church as completed in 1906 survives structurally unchanged, except for the roof of the south aisle. In 1952 the original lead covering was replaced by Westmorland slates, a change which certainly enhanced the appearance of the church. It is now certain that the remaining parts of Blomfield's design, the side chapel and north aisle, will never be built.

Internally there have been great changes to the furnishings. In the absence of the side chapel, a temporary Lady Chapel was fitted out at the east end of the south aisle in 1918, utilizing one of the medieval chests as an altar. In 1936 this was replaced by a permanent chapel designed by Thomas Spencer, a churchwarden and architect. Major changes occurred in 1979–80 when this chapel was dismantled and the pews, which dated back to 1866, were replaced by light oak benches, the object being to create a more flexible layout to accord with modern practice. To further this end, a nave altar was also introduced. The scheme also included a comprehensive restoration of the vestry house, the interior of which was in poor condition. This work considerably altered the north side of the church, as the upper floor of the vestry house was extended over the north aisle to the arcade, the top of which was glazed. Finally, two small additions were made on the north side of the church: a small vestry between the house and the organ transept, and a parish office on the west side of the house. The restoration of the vestry house provided two meeting rooms, designated the St Mary's and Wigan Rooms respectively, which provided some replacement for the Wigan Hall, which had been the parish hall until its closure in 1969.[1]

The extension of the vestry house into the church involved the removal of most of the north wall and many memorials being repositioned, mostly in the south aisle and the vestry house. Fortunately, only one of the historically important memorials was affected by these changes. The new rooms on the north side had the effect of blocking two windows surviving from 1840, both of which contained important glass. The window at the east end was retained, lit artificially, but the other at the west end was lost except for the top segment. However, this was offset by the restoration of the window at the east end of the south aisle, which also dates from 1840 and had been blocked since 1906.

The Church Today

The decision not to build the side chapel is to be regretted, not for itself but for the unfortunate effect it has on the chancel which is so much darker than the nave. Had the chapel been built, it would have been lit by light flooding through the arches and the general effect much improved. Sadly, modern liturgical

---

1 F. Mattingley, *The Frederick Wigan Trust Mortlake*, Barnes & Mortlake History Society, 1969.

practice makes the chancel less of a focus and, as it was not included in the 1979–80 remodelling, the contrast with the redecorated nave is unfortunate. No doubt in due time this will be remedied. If past history teaches us anything, it is that the present layout is transitory. A great gain from the 1980 changes was the restoration of the window at the east end of the south aisle which, coupled with the placement of memorial tablets, has given it an air of antiquity – a false air, but pleasant nonetheless. Outside, the unrendered brick on the south side remains to mark what might have been and to puzzle the casual pilgrim. The south aisle as built with its small neat porch, suits the nave well and is more in keeping with the modest churchyard than Blomfield's original design.

The Blomfield church, c. 1920. The temporary Lady Chapel is just visible in the south aisle.

8. THE PARISH SINCE 1840

The dramatic changes to the Parish Church after 1840 are mirrored in the parish. In 1840 it was still made up of the old village around the High Street, large estates in East Sheen and market gardens, although improving roads had reduced the attraction of East Sheen as a country retreat for City merchants. (For example, the Temple family had moved their country seat to Broadlands, near Romsey, in 1736, selling their East Sheen estate, Temple Grove, in 1808.) The catalyst that was to transform the parish to a modern London suburb was the opening of the Richmond Railway in 1846 and its subsequent extensions. As elsewhere around London, the railway enabled those who worked in the City to move out and fresh food could be brought in from a greater distance. By the latter part of the century, the estates and market gardens were of increasing value as building land for housing.

The development was gradual, but gathered momentum as the century progressed. It is illustrated by the rise in population. From about 1,800 in 1801 it increased to over 3,000 in 1851, before the railway can have had any effect, and then doubled to over 6,000 by 1881 and to 7,500 by 1901. It doubled again to 15,000 during the next ten years and after the First World War reached its present figure of about 20,000. Residential developments date from about 1850, characterized by small working-class cottages which were built around the church in Victoria Road, Vineyard Path and Church Path and south of the railway in the Queens Road area. Cottages also appeared in East Sheen, in Derby and Stanley Roads and in Christ Church Road near the 'Plough', although some of the latter are probably much earlier. Particularly interesting examples are Model Cottages and the very similar cottages in Wrights Walk. In addition, a number of large villas were built in East Sheen, of which Sir Frederick Wigan's Clare Lawn was perhaps the best known.

The break-up of the estates was heralded by the sale of the largest, Palewell Lodge, in 1896. Within a few years Palewell Park was laid out and, with the sale of Sheen House and Temple Grove a few years later, the Edwardian period saw many more roads made. The process reached its zenith between the two world wars when the market gardens were also built over and by 1939 the parish was largely as we know it. All but one of the eighteenth-century houses of East Sheen were swept away and most of the Victorian villas; Clare Lawn, for all its magnificence, stood for barely sixty years. Percy Lodge in Christ Church Road alone remains from the eighteenth century. Unfortunately, even in recent years more old and historic buildings have been demolished, not always for new housing; the west end of Mortlake High Street was lost to road-widening in the 1960s.

The first effect on the Church of these changes was a demand for a new church in the expanding area of East Sheen. It was first mooted in the 1850s, when Swinny was incumbent, but during the time of his successor, John Thomas Manley, the matter became urgent for Manley was an eloquent preacher and the Parish Church was filled to capacity. A building fund was opened in 1860 and Christ Church was consecrated in January 1864, after being delayed by the spectacular collapse of the tower during the building (fortunately without injury to anyone and not through any fault of the architect). A site on the Upper Richmond Road by the corner of Temple Sheen Road had been suggested, but others wanted it built further south on the hill towards Richmond Park. Since their subscriptions more than covered the cost of the site, their preference prevailed and Christ Church was built on a site as near the western boundary of the parish as the Parish Church was near the eastern. The new church seated about 525, increased to 650 when a north aisle was added in 1887, and undoubtedly eased pressure on the Parish Church.

By this time important changes were taking place both in and outside the Church. Under the influence of the Oxford Movement the sacraments regained their importance, with regular and frequent celebrations of the Holy Communion. At the same time the social convention that compelled church attendance was breaking down. The only guide to the number of people who attended services is the religious census of 1851, the figures for the Parish Church being given as 679 in the morning and 512 in the afternoon. In the 1860s when Manley was preaching, Anderson records that chairs had to be placed in the aisles; if the galleries were in full use, this indicates a congregation of over 1,300. Even allowing for the opening of Christ Church, these numbers soon declined to the point where the Parish Church could be rebuilt in 1905 with only 550 seats. Clearly, many of the new arrivals in the parish had no connection with the church and no desire for one. It was not only social and religious changes that affected services. Before the improvement in street lighting in the 1860s, Anderson recollects a lady who lived near the station, Miss Turner, having her way along Church Path lit by a page boy in buttons, while another family walked from Littleworth End with a lantern, which they put out in the porch and kept under the pew during the service.

The opening of Christ Church had another and far-reaching effect on the parish. The annual parish reports indicate that until the late 1870s the Parish Church offertories were considerably higher than those at Christ Church. In 1877 (the first time the combined offertories exceeded £1,000) they were £545 and £476 respectively. Despite this, the vicar, Albert Shutte, wrote in his report of a 'period of great anxiety and depression' and in 1878 of 'a year . . . full of anxiety and disquietude on every side and . . . commercial depression'. These anxieties seem to have affected the Parish Church congregation more than that of Christ Church, for in the following years the offertories declined markedly and from 1879 fell behind those of the daughter church. It was not until 1897 that the combined offertories again exceeded £1,000 and by then those at Christ Church were almost 40 per cent higher. Anderson refers to the social superiority of the more wealthy parishioners of East Sheen, manifested at this time with Christ Church becoming the 'fashionable' church and the Parish Church in its more working-class surroundings descending the social scale. It may be noted in this regard that pew rents were abolished at the Parish Church in the late 1890s,[1] whereas at Christ Church they survived until long after the Second World War. This social difference had no great effect while Horace Monroe and Edward Tupper were incumbents; the position of the Parish Church was maintained, as is illustrated by Monroe in 1912 persuading Frank Figg, organist at Christ Church since 1888, to take the 'more senior' post at the Parish Church.

By the early 1900s it was clear that a third church was needed in the rapidly expanding area north of the Upper Richmond Road, which had been almost entirely given over to market gardens. The first mention is in 1902 when the vicar, Walter Furneaux, wrote in the parish magazine that a site had been promised in the Lower Richmond Road near the old West End School (by Manor Road). Nothing further materialized and it was the new vicar in 1909, Horace Monroe, who made the provision of a second church one of his main aims. A fund was launched in 1912 for a church in Clifford Avenue, but the First World War prevented much progress. In 1919 the parish was offered a site on the old Palewell estate, then being developed. The new church project was transferred to that site and in 1929 All Saints was built and consecrated. It provided some colour in the parish; until then the prevailing churchmanship had been Low, but at the new church vestments and incense were soon introduced. The erection of this church was the achievement of Edward Tupper, who had succeeded Monroe as vicar, and he also opened another church, St Andrew's. This was an army hut from Bramshot Camp, erected on the site in Clifford Avenue in 1921. It was a temporary expedient while All Saints was built, but the temporary became permanent. The economic situation in the 1930s and a dwindling congregation after the Second World War made it clear that a permanent church would not be built, but St Andrew's remained until January 1975 when it closed, the hut having reached the end of its useful life.

Reference has been made to the social rivalry between Mortlake and East Sheen, exacerbated by the larger financial support for the parish coming from Christ Church. This did not matter while the parish had a sufficient staff of clergy. From the time it was built, All Saints had a priest-in-charge, while the vicar and assistant curates cared for the Parish Church, Christ Church and St Andrew's. During and after the Second World War, the staffing situation was such that, while All Saints retained a priest-in-charge, the incumbent had only himself to cover the other three churches with assistance from an occasional curate and such other clergy as were willing to take Sunday services. In the circumstances, the ageing vicar gave his prime attention to Christ Church and was seldom seen at the Parish Church, where for much of the 1950s a local doctor was in charge. The congregational life at the Parish Church inevitably suffered

---

1 Although abolished in the 1890s, pew rents were still being paid in the 1920s by holders allotted pews thirty years before.

and was at a low ebb when Samuel Erskine succeeded Glyn Lewis in 1960. The new vicar was, like his predecessor, obliged to be at Christ Church more often than elsewhere, but he built up a team of young assistant curates, two of whom were responsible for the Parish Church, which recovered remarkably quickly after its years of neglect. When Bernard Jacob became vicar in 1968, the incumbent was once again seen in his Parish Church.

A most important change came to the parish with the introduction in January 1976 of a team ministry. Under the scheme Christ Church and All Saints each had a team vicar, with the incumbent as rector and leader of the team, with particular responsibility for the Parish Church. It was from this time that the Parish Church began to be regularly referred to by its dedication, probably for the first time in its history.

The Parish Boundaries

Until about 1890 the parish boundaries ran down the centre of White Hart Lane, along Beverley Brook and into Richmond Park, westwards through Pen Ponds, south from the Sidmouth Plantation to Pesthouse Common, along Manor Road, the east side of Sandycombe Lane and back to the river along the west side of the railway embankment to Kew railway bridge. Thus a large part of the parish, 732 acres, or nearly a third, is in Richmond Park. Its enclosure by Charles I in 1637 aroused considerable anger, but the King paid for the land and the owners eventually sold. As a result, both White Lodge and Bog Lodge are in the parish. It will be noted that in 1890 the parish also included what is now North Sheen and Kew, including Kew Gardens station. In 1894 the transfer of that area to Richmond was approved by Parliament despite the opposition of Mortlake. The parish was reduced by 329 acres, mostly market gardens.

The Diocese

For many centuries the parish was within the diocese of Winchester, but the latter had no jurisdiction;[2] even after the archbishops left, the parish remained a Peculiar of the Archbishop of Canterbury, attached to the Rural Deanery of Croydon and Shoreham. In 1845 Mortlake ceased to be a Peculiar and was transferred to the diocese of London. In 1876, in an attempt to reorganize the large and unwieldy dioceses, Mortlake was transferred to Rochester and in 1905 was included in the new diocese of Southwark.

---

2 In 1799 the Bishop of Winchester did consecrate the churchyard extension.

Mortlake High Street in the early years of this century. The buildings were demolished in the 1950s. Note the gates at the entrance to Church Path, by which two gentlemen are talking.

The Blomfield nave in 1969 with the Wigan memorial over the west door.

30

9. THE TOWER

The tower is the only part of the church to survive from 1543 and its history is entirely separate from the main body of the church, whose many changes have left it untouched. Unfortunately, it has been subject to a serious historical misconception, namely that only the lower three storeys date from 1543, the belfry being added when the bells were installed in 1694 and the cupola a few years later. It was Yeandle[1] who first put forward the proposition in his otherwise excellent book, but in fairness he did say the belfry was 'thought to have been added'. Later historians have converted the thought into fact without producing evidence for it.

There is nothing either in the vestry records or a critical examination of the tower to support the theory. It would appear that Yeandle made the assumption solely on the basis that the brickwork of the belfry is clearly later than 1543, without examining the interior. Had he and later writers done so, they would have found the belfry lined with brick earlier than 1694. In addition, there were four bells prior to 1694 which could not have been hung anywhere else in the tower; the lower storey has no sound outlets and the stair turret on the north side extends in Tudor brick to the roof and cupola.

The tower is of considerable interest. Sixteenth-century towers are rare, but at first sight the lower stages are not what one would expect in a Tudor tower. As discussed in chapter 2, the church was reconstructed from the materials of the old church which stood by the manor house and it is these lower stages of the tower which provide the evidence for this. The ashlar and flint work is typical of the early fifteenth century, but after completing the second stage little good stone seems to have been left, for in the third stage the stonework is much less regular. Indeed, inside the tower tiles can be seen inserted, presumably to line up the layers of uneven stone. Further evidence is provided by the turret on the north side of the tower, which contained the staircase. The base is of stone, but about 10 feet or so from the ground it becomes Tudor brick, which continues to the roof. The problem with the fourth, belfry, stage is not whether it dates from 1543, but what its original form was before reconstruction. The earliest prints of the church from the eighteenth century differ in detail, but all agree in showing the tower as an entity; there is no evidence that the top stage was in any way different from the rest of the tower. There is the brick lining which has been much altered (mutilated perhaps would be a better description), but some of the bricks at least appear to be Tudor. The most likely explanation is that there was so little stone left that this stage was built in brick with a stone facing.

---

1 W. H. Yeandle, *The History of the Churches in Mortlake and East Sheen*, R. W. Simpson & Co. Ltd., 1925, p. 8.

Above the belfry was a battlemented parapet and the most distinctive feature of Mortlake church, the cupola. There can be little doubt that this is an original feature. Whilst it was not unusual for bell cotes or turrets to be added to towers around the eighteenth century, they tended to be modest affairs, removed later when maintenance became a nuisance. (Richmond and Twickenham parish churches are examples where this occurred.) The cupola at Mortlake is not a modest structure. The base is a small room 8 feet 9 inches by 7 feet 6 inches and 6 feet 6 inches high, with an inside height of 7 feet 6 inches, the floor being countersunk into the tower roof. Above, the lantern is approximately 10 feet high. A structure of such size and weight could not have been added to the tower without major alterations to the tower roof, for which there is no evidence. Steel girders now bear the weight, but the original timber beams are still in place and, although they have not been dated, they appear to be far older than the eighteenth century.

It was in 1795–6 that the tower assumed its present form when the belfry stage was refaced in stock brick with a plain parapet. A vestry minute of 12 October 1795 states 'Church Steeple ordered to be repaired', but the accounts in the churchwardens' ledger indicate it was nothing less than a complete restoration. The total cost of the work was £194.1s.6d. and included in that sum were large payments to the bricklayer, stonemason and carpenter. Clearly, the work covered far more than refacing the belfry. There are frequent references to other repairs to the tower, but the only other major work was in 1950 when the top stage of the stair turret had to be renewed after a crack developed in it.

Two interesting developments affected the tower in the middle of the last century. In 1850, when heating was first installed in the church, the problem of a boiler-house arose. It was solved by making use of the deep foundations under the tower, the boiler being put in under the base of the stair turret, the turret itself becoming the flue. This involved removing the spiral staircase, access to the tower in future being by a series of ladders, which is no doubt the reason why Yeandle and other historians never inspected the inside of the tower. A few years later, in about 1865, the architect replaced the arch in the west door in the course of some repairs. Anderson relates that his father was churchwarden at the time and was so annoyed he ordered the old arch to be erected in the churchyard, where it remains.[2] (We cannot but admire the imperiousness of the Victorian churchwarden!)

The cupola in its very exposed position must have called for constant attention, and it is extremely doubtful whether any sixteenth-century timber survives. Some of the timbers in the base are of deal and appear to be second-hand. In the vestry minutes for May 1787 are details of timber for a new bell frame, including 'two 10 foot whole deals and 5 foot of double deal'. There can be little doubt that is what is now in the cupola. The last, very thorough restoration was carried out in 1988–9 when English Heritage was among the bodies that contributed to the cost. Had Sir Arthur Blomfield's plans for the church been fully implemented, this stage of the tower would have been rebuilt with tall pinnacles. Whilst the

2 J. E. Anderson, 'Mortlake Memories', unpublished memoirs.

stock brick of 1795 may not be very attractive, the tower would have been much less interesting had this been done.

A feature of some turn-of-the-century pictures of the tower is the ivy. It first seems to have appeared on the tower around 1860 and by 1900 almost completely enveloped it. That may look picturesque, but it can do untold damage to the walls. It was later cut back, although not removed until 1930.

The Bells

The first mention of bells is in the inventory of church goods prepared by the commissioners of Edward VI in 1552. This listed three bells in the steeple, together with a 'saunze', or sanctus bell. Since this was only nine years after the church was built, it is probably reasonable to assume they came from the old church. We have no other information about them, although the vestry minutes frequently refer to them. One of the early entries in the minutes for 1580 records:

> Itm. Payd to Ringers for rinnginge at the quenes remove
> frome Richemon . . . vid

In 1694 the ring[3] was augmented to six bells, at least that is what the Vestry thought happened. However, the founders' invoice in the churchwardens' accounts makes clear that six bells were supplied, credit being given for the three old bells. (There is no reference here or later to the sanctus bell, which was most likely removed during the Commonwealth.) Philip Whiteman of Clerkenwell was the founder, five of the bells being dated 1694, and the sixth 1695, from which one deduces that he cast the ring in the last weeks of 1694 but did not finish the tenor until the New Year. There is nothing in the vestry minutes until July 1695, when a security was given on church lands for £150 to 'pay for ye bells'. From subsequent entries, it is clear the parish did not have any money and £150, later increased to £180, was borrowed from a churchwarden, Richard Adams, to whom the security was given. The remainder of the cost, another £100, was paid by Samuel Meredith. Who Meredith was we do not know and we know very little of Richard Adams except that his family were market gardeners for several generations. When Adams died in 1703 the parish had to repay the debt to his widow, which indicates that he was of sufficient substance not to have enforced repayment during his life. Payment to his widow was made by making over the rents from the 'Garter property' (the 'Star & Garter', formerly Church House, next to the 'Ship' on Thames Bank).

Having got a ring of six bells, the ringers' thoughts now turned to augmenting the ring to eight bells. In June 1741 a vestry minute records:

> The Churchwardens and others named, or any 5 to be at
> liberty to agree with Robert Catlin or any other person to
> cast two new Trebles and new hang them with ye old 6
> Bells, and which is to be compleated without any rate upon
> ye Parish.

---

3   A ring is the correct term for a collection of bells; a peal is what is rung on them.

The new bells were cast in 1746 by Thomas Lester at what is now the Whitechapel Bell Foundry. They were presented by Theodore Eccleston (1715–53) of Crowfield Hall, Suffolk, and Mortlake, who was a noted ringer and patron of the Exercise (the term still used to describe English bellringing). In addition to Mortlake, he gave bells to Stonham Aspall in Suffolk, to Winchester Cathedral and to All Saints, Fulham. He lived in Mortlake High Street, his house being on the site of John Dee's opposite the church. He must have been a man of considerable wealth, but his life was dogged by sorrow. He was married at Mortlake in 1746, hence no doubt the gift of bells, and a son was born the following year. However, his wife died in childbirth in 1748, his son in 1751 and Eccleston himself in 1753 when he was only thirty-eight. All the family were buried in the churchyard, but the tomb has been lost.

One of the Whiteman bells had to be recast by Robert Catlin of Holborn in 1751. According to the inscription this was 'by subscription of the Ringers', but again it would appear to have been largely paid for by Eccleston. In 1783 one of the trebles given by Eccleston was cracked in an accident. This time a sub-scription list was opened and the bell re-cast by Thomas Janaway of Chelsea in 1784. So the bells remain today. There has been much attention to their fittings over the years, notably in 1911 when the present cast-iron frame was put in and in 1978–9 when the bells were re-hung with new fittings. The ring is notable for being one of the very few eight-bell rings surviving in its original condition from the seventeenth and eighteenth centuries and its tone is remarkably good for bells of that age. It is also a large ring for the tower, the tenor weighing 14½ hundredweight.

The Clock

The first mention of a clock is in the vestry records for 1712:

> May ye 6th Pd. Wm. Jones for Bringing up ye £43 ye Gift
> of Mr. Matthew Deacker for ye Clock & Cupillo. . 1s. 6d.

There follows a second entry which indicates that there was a problem with the gift:

> May 19th Churchwardens to procure an addition of halfe
> a hunderweight to the Bell for ye clock, the gift
> of Mr. Deakers, and another hand on the south
> side of the clock, and to pay for ye gilding ye ball
> and vaine upon ye cubito by writeing ye name
> of Mr. Deakers in gold letters.

From these entries, it would seem Mr. Deacker or Deakers gave Mortlake a gift of a clock, but that it proved insufficient to cover the cost and the parish had to make up the difference. The references suggest the benefactor was not local, indeed had he been he would surely have relieved the parish of its embarrassment. There is no further reference to him in connection with Mortlake. As to his identity, the only candidate seems to be Sir Matthew Decker (1679–1749), buried in Richmond Parish Church, whose memorial is so prominent against the north wall of the church. Why this noted eighteenth-century resident of Richmond was so generous to Mortlake we do not know.[4]

The clock was installed in the stage under the bells, with the clock bell in the cupola. The bell remains, inscribed with the date 1712, but the clock itself was replaced in 1838 by the present clock, made by John Moore & Son of Clerkenwell.

The Weathercock

The fine weathercock on top of the cupola has been dated as early eighteenth century and was restored with the cupola in 1989. There is not much in the vestry records, but under 1678–9 is the entry:

Pd. John Emerson for a weathercock on ye Steeple . . 7s. 0d.

There seems no reason to doubt that it is the same weathercock.

North view of the church, 1992.

4   James Green, 'Fitzwilliam House or Pembroke Lodge on Richmond Green', *Richmond History*, Journal of the Richmond Local History Society, 1988, p. 59.

What might have been! A sketch of Sir Arthur Blomfield's original design. (From the restoration appeal leaflet in 1904.)

10. THE CHURCHYARD

[A full history of the churchyard until the restoration of 1983 will be found in *The Story of Mortlake Churchyard* by Richard Jeffree, Barnes & Mortlake History Society, 1983]

The small churchyard surrounding the 1543 church was enlarged in 1742 and is shown in the earliest prints with a low wall and a stile across Church Path. It was enlarged again in 1799 to its present form; the path through the arch marks the boundary of 1742, and until 1842 it ran across to Tinderbox Alley. The churchyard was closed for burials at the end of 1854 and the railings along Church Path were erected about that time. Interments in some family tombs were exempted from the closure order, the last burial being in the Penrhyn tomb in 1919. Responsibility for the churchyard's maintenance passed to the local council in the 1920s, but it only carried out basic tidying. During the Second World War the railings round many of the tombs were removed, but fortunately not those round the churchyard itself.

In 1957 Barnes Council considered turning the churchyard into a recreation ground. This proposal was followed over the years by other schemes to landscape the churchyard, all of which envisaged the removal of most of the tombs and headstones. In addition, the Parochial Church Council at one stage contemplated a church hall in the south-east corner. By great good fortune, none of these schemes came to fruition, the only work undertaken being in 1960 when the High Street was widened and the buildings backing on to the churchyard were demolished. These sites were partly taken into the churchyard, which at the same time was tidied and some tombs cleaned. Nothing more was done and during the 1970s its overall condition deteriorated until it was utterly derelict, with most of the tombs in poor condition, some ruinous.

In 1983 an appeal was launched by the Mortlake Community Association, with the support of the Parochial Church Council and the Barnes & Mortlake History Society, to restore the churchyard in accordance with a scheme drawn up by Allan Hart, a local landscape architect. The scheme was approved by the local council, by then the London Borough of Richmond upon Thames, with their agreement to match the amount raised by the appeal. Work commenced in April 1984, and was completed in 1986.

The architect's design proved one of the most successful schemes of its type. All the major tombs were retained *in situ* and repaired, together with a large number of the upright stones where their condition allowed, although some were re-positioned. A major achievement of the scheme was to retain the essential feel of a churchyard, yet at the same time make it a place of rest and enjoyment in a way it had never been before. Repairs were carried out to all the surviving table tombs. In the case of Alderman John Barber this was only made possible by the efforts of Henry Shearman, a former churchwarden who, with the assistance of the rector, Ian Cundy, retrieved the stone facings scattered over the churchyard shortly before the contractors started work; but for this, the facings would almost certainly have been lost in clearing the debris from the churchyard and it would have been impossible to restore one of its important tombs.

Maintenance of the churchyard is now vested with the friends of Mortlake Churchyard. This restoration ranks as one of the comparatively rare improvements in this century which have been an unqualified benefit to Mortlake and its people.

Alderman.John Barber (1676–1741). Lord Mayor of London 1733.

The nave and chancel, 1978. Note the Lady Chapel erected in 1936, the pews of 1866 and the Coventry memorial.

The fifteenth-century font present by Archbishop Thomas Bourchier.

Late fifteenth-century chest, probably made in south Germany.

11. ORNAMENTS, FURNITURE AND MEMORIALS

The Font
The oldest relic in the church and the only object we have from the old church is a very fine font, albeit somewhat battered from five hundred years of use. It was given by Thomas Bourchier (1405–86), who was Archbishop of Canterbury from 1454 until his death. His archiepiscopate covered the last part of the War of the Roses and he crowned three kings, Edward IV, Richard III and Henry VII. He is remembered as a man of culture and a great builder: he rebuilt his house at Knole, and there is evidence that he was often at Mortlake and rebuilt the manor house. The octagonal bowl of the font is decorated with various devices and one panel embodies a cardinal's hat, which provides a clue to the date of the font. (Bourchier was made a cardinal in 1465.) In 1725 the Vestry ordered its removal, but fortunately rescinded the order the following year.

Medieval Chests
There are three such chests in the church. One with a semi-hexagonal lid is English, probably from the first half of the sixteenth century; a second iron-bound chest, with an elaborate lock in the lid, is German. (A note in the vestry minutes records that a chest was bought in 1617 for the 'Regester Booke'. It could be this one.) The greatest interest attaches to the third chest, often erroneously referred to as an 'Armada' chest. Made of walnut, inlaid with ebony and boxwood, it is a superb example of medieval woodwork. It is in fine condition, with its original hinges, and the inside of the lid is embellished with tinned ironwork, backed with red cloth and velvet. It has been dated to the late fifteenth century and the provenance was probably South Germany. How it came into the church we do not know, but, as with the others, it seems to have been sometime in the seventeenth century.

Silver
The church has a fine collection of Restoration silver, which is not suitable for day-to-day use and can only be displayed on rare occasions. It consists of a chalice and paten dated 1660, a pair of flagons from 1681 and an alms-dish dated 1687. A contrast is provided by the modern altar-cross and candlesticks designed and made by Omar Ramsden of Chelsea in 1936. They are the parishioners' memorial to Edward Heathfield Tupper (vicar, 1918–30), a handsome memorial which reflects the high regard and affection in which he was held. Although still in regular use, they are not kept on display.

The Nave and Chancel Furniture

Except for two high-backed seventeenth-century chairs in the chancel, all the fittings date from after the rebuilding of 1885 and, being factory-produced, they are not of great artistic or historical interest. The fittings associated with the nave altar and the benches are the most recent, installed in 1980. The Victorian and Edwardian fittings were mostly given as memorials, for example, the reredos is a composite memorial given in 1890 and the pulpit was subscribed for in 1902 as a memorial to Albert Shutte (vicar, 1865–95).

The Windows

There is not a great deal of stained glass in the church and what there is is mainly Victorian or Edwardian. Two windows are, however, of some interest. That at the east end of the north aisle is the oldest glass in the church. It depicts 'The Road to Emmaus' and was given in 1867 by Mrs James Wigan in memory of her brother, Rev. W. Harman Nicholls. It is lit artificially, having been covered by the small vestry added in 1980. The other glass is in the east window of the south aisle and was given in 1937 in memory of Thomas Leaney, headmaster of the National or Church Schools from 1869 to 1913. It too was originally in the north aisle and was moved to its present position in 1980.

The Organ

The first organ, built by W. Allen, was installed in the west gallery in 1840. In 1885 it was moved to the new organ transept and in 1899 Hill & Sons (successors to W. Allen) built the present organ to the design of Dr C. S. Jekyll.[1] The new organ incorporated some pipework from the old organ, but is a much larger instrument constructed on the 'tubular pneumatic' system. It has only recently received a thorough cleaning and restoration.

The Altar-Piece, 'The Entombment of Christ'

A prominent feature of the church for nearly two hundred years, this was presented by Benjamin Vandergucht, a Dutch picture-dealer, in 1794 and was in the chancel until 1851, when it was banished to the vestry. In 1918 it was set up in the south aisle as part of the temporary Lady Chapel, but when a permanent chapel was erected in 1936 it went back to the vestry. There it remained until it was sold in 1979. Although attributed to Gerhad Seghers (1592–1651), expert opinion is now that it came from the Reubens studio.

Memorials

HON. FRANCIS COVENTRY (1612–1700)

Without doubt, this is the outstanding memorial in the church. A large and impressive caryatid design, it is on the east wall of the south aisle, but until 1840 was on the south wall of the chancel. Coventry was not a notable man, being the second son by a second marriage of the Rt. Hon. Thomas, Lord Coventry, Baron

1 Organist 1897–1905, formerly organist and composer to the Chapels Royal.

Sir Philip Francis (1740–1818).

Henry Addington, 1st Lord Sidmouth (1757–1844). Prime Minister 1801–4.

of Alsboroug (Aylesborough), who was Lord Keeper of the Great Seal of England to Charles I. The fame of the memorial lies in its sculptor, William Kidwell (1664–1736), the leading English sculptor of his time. Much of his work is in Ireland, but the Mortlake monument is by common consent his finest achievement.

NICHOLAS AND SARAH GODSCHALL (died 1748 and 1750)

A fine eighteenth-century memorial by an unknown sculptor. It is notable for the inscription, a glowing account of the Christian virtues of Nicholas and Sarah. The Godschalls were City merchants engaged in the Turkey trade who came from Flanders and lived at The Firs, an eighteenth-century house which stood in Sheen Lane. (It was demolished after being badly damaged by a 'Flying Bomb' in 1944.)

SIR PHILIP FRANCIS (1740–1818)

Historically this is the most important memorial in the church. Sir Philip was reputed to be the author of the 'Letters of Junius', which ferociously attacked the monarch, ministers and public men of the day. He was a clerk in the War Office and went to India in 1773, where he developed a bitter relationship with Warren Hastings, with whom he fought a duel. He seems to have been a very sour man, but returned from India in 1780 with a fortune. He became an MP in 1784 and was knighted under the Regency. He lived at East Sheen Lodge from 1783 to 1805, a house which stood in Sheen Lane on the site of Hood Avenue. The memorial was moved to its position over the south door in 1980; previously it was in the vestry.

SIR BROOK WATSON (1735–1807)

As an orphan Watson went to sea and at the age of fourteen lost a leg in an encounter with a shark off Havana. He served with Wolfe in Canada and in 1782 was made Commissary-General to the Army. He took up residence at The Cedars in East Sheen in 1780. (The house stood on the site of Cedar Court in Sheen Lane.) During the years he lived here he became a leading figure in the City, a director of the Bank of England 1784–1807, Chairman of Lloyds 1796–1806 and Lord Mayor in 1796, reputedly the only Lord Mayor with a wooden leg. He was created a baronet in 1803 and Lord Liverpool spoke of him as 'one of the most honourable men ever known'. His tomb on the north side of the church was taken into the church in the 1816 alterations, but a flat stone marks its position in the north aisle, close to a memorial designed by Sir Edwin Cooper which was erected by Lloyds as recently as 1939.

HENRY ADDINGTON, 1st LORD SIDMOUTH (1757–1844)

The memorial is quite close to the Brook Watson memorial. Addington was Speaker of the House of Commons 1789–1801, Prime Minister 1801–4, Lord President of the Council 1805 and 1812, and Home Secretary 1812. A sound administrator, very conservative in his views, his premiership was undistinguished but, however history may view him, Henry Addington gives distinction to Mortlake; few parish churches boast a memorial to a prime minister. He was created a viscount in 1805. George III granted him White Lodge in Richmond Park as his residence in 1801, and he lived there until his death in 1844. After retiring from political life, he devoted himself to Park affairs. Appointed Deputy Ranger in 1813, he did much to repair the neglect of the eighteenth century. He enclosed the garden round White Lodge and the Sidmouth plantation is a reminder of his work. He is buried in the churchyard in the vault built for his first wife, Ursula Mary, who died in 1811. She has a notable memorial on the west wall, although its position rather high on the wall makes it difficult to view. The sculptor was Sir Richard Westmacott (1775–1856) who was made an RA in 1811. The 1840 print of the church shows that its original position was on the north wall of the old chancel.

SIR FRANCIS MOLYNEUX OMMANNEY (1774–1840)

Navy Agent and banker of Norfolk Street, off the Strand, Sir Francis was one of the most influential parishioners and benefactors in the first part of the nineteenth century. He had a large family of whom several had connections with the parish. One son was incumbent in the 1830s, but it was his eighth son, Octavius, who followed his father in the business and who likewise was prominent in parish affairs until retiring in 1870. He was much involved in the building of Christ Church and was one of its first churchwardens (at the same time he was also churchwarden at the Parish Church). He is commemorated by a plaque in the south aisle at Christ Church, but has no memorial at the Parish Church.

JAMES WIGAN (1832–1902)

In the latter part of the nineteenth century the Wigan family was one of the most important in the parish. The brothers Sir Frederick and James were arguably the most benevolent supporters the parish has known. Frederick went into the Southwark hop business founded by his grandfather; his younger brother James was apprenticed as a brewer and in 1852 went into partnership with Charles Phillips at Mortlake. In 1877 he left the partnership and purchased a brewery at Bishops Stortford, but continued to live in Mortlake at Cromwell House. In 1905 the nave of the Parish Church was rebuilt in his memory, and after his wife Maria died in 1918, their thirteen children erected the striking mural monument over the west door of the church.

JOHN DEE (1527–1608)

The most celebrated resident of Mortlake has no memorial. Since his death, he has tended to be regarded as little more than a wizard or necromancer, but modern research is restoring his standing as one of the foremost scholars of the Renaissance and a mathematician who has had few equals. He came to Mortlake in 1566 and lived opposite the church, where he was visited on at least two occasions by Elizabeth I.

Sir Brook Watson (1735–1807). Lord Mayor of London 1796.

John Dee (1527–1608).

12. THE VESTRY

The Vestry evolved from the officers appointed by the parishioners to be responsible for the church possessions, the churchwardens being the principal officers. When the Tudors and Stuarts made the parish the basic unit of local government what had been a purely religious body evolved as the local authority. By the nineteenth century the imperfections of the system were such that in 1866 many of the civic duties were transferred to other bodies, finally being vested in authorities set up under the Local Government Act of 1894. The Vestries again became purely religious but, under changes made in 1919–21 in the way the Church of England was governed, they were replaced by Parochial Church Councils. From at least 1676 the Mortlake Vestry met in the vestry house. The Parochial Church Council still does and can thus claim to have met in the same building for nearly 320 years.

The transactions of the Vestry were recorded in minute books and in the churchwardens' accounts. We are very fortunate that in the case of Mortlake these records have survived to a large extent intact since about 1575. They constitute the largest and most complete collection of parish records in the Surrey Record Office. The records present a fascinating jumble of the sacred and the secular. The earliest entries are taken up in the main by payments to beggars and vagrants of all descriptions, and implementation of the later Poor Laws must have been particularly onerous. In the eighteenth century the records reach their zenith in completeness and detail. During the nineteenth century they take on a modern, businesslike appearance and in consequence become far less interesting.

As the duties of the Vestry increased, the office of Vestry Clerk must have increased in importance. At Mortlake the first record of a clerk being appointed is in 1674 and there were several notable holders of the office. William Woolfe held the office for fifty-five years from 1774 and is commemorated in the church. Charles King (1773–1856) was clerk from 1828 to 1855 and may well have been responsible for the preservation of so many of the records. In 1854 the Vestry resolved to enter all the parish papers in a book and index them, possibly at the prompting of King. He lived at Suthrey House in Mortlake High Street and was an aspiring but not very successful architect. He was the drawing master at Miss Crabtree's school in East Sheen and was also in charge of the 'Mortlake Volunteers' formed in 1805 during the Napoleonic invasion scare. It earned him the sobriquet 'Captain King'. There is no memorial to this great Mortlake character, but several of his drawings still exist, notably a lovely view of Mortlake riverfront in 1830.

The last Vestry Clerks were Eustace Anderson (1819–1889) and his son, John Eustace Anderson (1844–1915). Both were solicitors. Eustace Anderson was churchwarden at the Parish Church in the 1860s (he was responsible for the arch being erected in the churchyard) and was appointed Vestry Clerk in 1867. His son succeeded him in the post in 1889 and was also Clerk to Barnes Urban District Council 1893–1911 and solicitor to the Council from 1911. On his death in 1915 the office of Vestry Clerk was abolished. It is difficult to exaggerate the debt we owe John Eustace Anderson, not only for ensuring the vestry records were kept intact, but for his own writings on local history. He built up a considerable local collection, including several thousand prints of Surrey. They were sold after his death, but some were saved by the vicar, Horace Monroe, and form the basis of the print collection at the Parish Church, while a number of other prints are in the local collection in Richmond Reference Library.

Church Path, 1968. The Church school to the left, a corner shop and a distant view of the Parish Church. A typical Mortlake view.

13. THE PARSON AND THE PARSONAGE

The earliest patron of the living was presumably the Archbishop of Canterbury as lord of the manor. In 1536 the patron became the Crown when the manor passed to Henry VIII. He retained the patronage when he gave the manor to Catherine Parr in 1544, and in 1546 granted it to the Dean and Chapter of Worcester. The intention was that the latter would declare the living a vicarage, but the King died before the grant took effect. Edward VI renewed the grant but reserved the rights to the Crown should a vicarage be declared. Not surprisingly, the Dean and Chapter let the living remain a perpetual curacy, to which a priest was licensed, not inducted, and the stipend was fixed at a specified figure. During the Commonwealth Mortlake was briefly a rectory, but at the Restoration reverted to a perpetual curacy, which it remained until a statute of 1868 made it possible to style such incumbents vicars and enabled a long-overdue improvement to the stipend. Under the team ministry introduced in 1976 the incumbent is styled rector, but the Dean and Chapter of Worcester remain the legal patrons.

Unfortunately, we know nothing of the incumbents before the seventeenth century. The first we have a note of is Francis Kitchen in 1603. He died in 1617 and has been followed by:

1617	George Langford
1633	Job Tookie
1637	George Harrison
1638	John Robinson – sequestered 1651
1655	Robert Parkes
1657	David Clarkson – rector 1658; ejected for Nonconformity 1662
1662	Robert Anderson
1671	Joseph Thompson
1678	William Hopkins
1681	William Jones
1720	William Bramston, DD
1735	Philip Smalridge
1751	Thomas Cornthwaite
1799	Septimus Collinson, DD
1813	Edward Owen
1820	Edward James
1832	Edward Aislabie Ommanney
1841	Frederick John Hawkes Reeves
1850	Henry Hutchinson Swinny
1855	John Thomas Manley
1863	Lawrence John Harrison

1865   Albert Shadwell Shutte – vicar from 1868
1896   Walter Coplestone Furneaux
1909   Horace Granville Monroe
1918   Edward Heathfield Tupper
1931   Hywel Glyn-Lewis
1940   Charles E. Douglas – priest-in-charge
1945   Hywel Glyn-Lewis
1960   Samuel Thomas Erskine
1968   Bernard Victor Jacob – rector from 1976
1978   Ian Patrick Martyn Cundy
1984   Bruce Alexander Saunders

A poorly paid perpetual curacy was hardly a sought-after appointment, so it is hardly surprising the list of incumbents contains few names of note. David Clarkson is the outstanding figure of the earlier incumbents. He was one of the chief literary champions of Nonconformity and an able preacher. After his ejection, he continued to live in Mortlake and in 1672 was licensed to preach to the Presbyterians and Congregationalists. He is generally considered one of the founders of the local Congregational church. William Jones lived in the parish, but the later seventeenth- and eighteenth-century incumbents were pluralists and were seldom, if ever, seen in Mortlake. Of the nineteenth-century incumbents, James, Ommanney and Reeves were all related to local families; John Manley was a noted preacher, but the most notable was Henry Hutchinson Swinny. In 1859 he became Principal of Cuddesdon Theological College and, but for ill-health and an early death, would probably have received further preferment. He was as near a High Churchman as the parish has ever had.

The twentieth-century incumbents have made more of a mark. Horace Monroe and Samuel Erskine were both notable vicars at difficult times and became canons of Southwark and Chelmsford Cathedrals respectively. Bernard Jacob was appointed archdeacon, first of Kingston and later of Reigate, and in 1992 Ian Cundy was consecrated bishop suffragan of Lewes, the first incumbent of the parish to be raised to bishops' orders.

The Parsonage

The original parsonage stood near the west end of Mortlake High Street on the north side, close to the tithe barn. The odd business of the Vestry first designating and then rescinding the use of the vestry house as the minister's house in 1670 may indicate the old house was not entirely suitable, but it probably remained in use as such until the death of William Jones in 1720. It had certainly fallen out of use by 1780 and incumbents, or resident ministers, had to find their own houses until 1867 when a vicarage was built on a plot in Stonehill Field (now Vicarage Road).[1] It was enlarged in 1896–7 and remained in use as the vicarage until 1955. It was then sold, being too large for modern conditions, and 248 Sheen Lane

1   Fortunately, the nineteenth-century incumbents seem to have been of independent means. Swinny, for example, resided at The Limes in Mortlake High Street.

purchased in its stead. That in turn was sold in 1981 and the rectory moved to 170 Sheen Lane.

The old vicarage in Vicarage Road was converted into flats after its sale and is now called Mortlake House. Its external appearance has not changed greatly and it is one of the few large Victorian houses to survive in East Sheen.

David Clarkson (1622–86). Leading Nonconformist divine and incumbent 1657–62.

BIBLIOGRAPHY

Anderson, J. E. *A History of the Parish of Mortlake*, 1886 (facsimile edition with amendments, 1983)

Gill, R. C. *A Dictionary of Local Celebrities*, 1980

Gill, R. C. & Mattingley, F. *Christ Church East Sheen – A Centenary History*, 1963

Hailstone, H. C. *The Alleyways of Mortlake and East Sheen*, 1983

Jeffree, R. *The Story of Mortlake Churchyard*, 1983

Lysons, D. *The Environs of London*, 1791–6

Yeandle, W. H. & Watts, W. W. *The History of the Churches in Mortlake and East Sheen*, 1925

Parish Reports and Parish Magazines at the Surrey Record Office, Kingston

Manuscript and Unpublished Sources

Anderson, J. E. 'Mortlake Memories'

Mortlake Vestry minutes and papers and churchwardens' accounts at the Surrey Record Office, Kingston.

INDEX